Julian + Carol

Just in case you don't
know how to do it properly.

Congratulations on

Your Engagement

Robert + Jane
+ Fred.

GW00771293

GETTING MARRIED

GETTING MARRIED

A Guide to Planning Weddings

Mary Gostelow

B T BATSFORD LTD
LONDON

ISBN 0 7134 4880 6

Typeset by Progress Filmsetting
and printed in Great Britain by
Butler Tanner Ltd
Frome, Somerset
for the publishers
B T Batsford Ltd
4 Fitzhardinge Street
London W1H 0AH

CONTENTS

INTRODUCTION

You may think there are many books and magazines for brides and others concerned with weddings. You may think that you already know everything there is to know—but when it comes to the point and you are actually involved in a wedding, to a greater or lesser extent, you may *panic*.

This guidebook shows you how you can cope without fuss. Whether you are bride, mother or guest, *Getting Married* provides you with practical guidance for the wedding of today.

I hope you enjoy reading and using the book as much as I have enjoyed compiling it.

I should especially like to thank the man to whom I am married, Martin Gostelow, and also my partner Wendy Lees, and the other people who have been particularly helpful: Sarah Appleby; Hilary Close; Andrew Fraser; Kay Harding; Richard Furnival Jones; Lisa Richards; Nicky Roberts; Jenny Turton and Ann Wardill (Harrods); Anne Beckwith-Smith, Lady-in-Waiting to HRH The Princess of Wales; Allison Guertin; Dulcie House; Jane Howard (Kingsway Public Relations); Ann Janin; Nancy Jarratt and Henri Perrier Moët (Moët & Chandon); Laurence Isaacson and Ralph Taylor (Maxim's de Paris); Diana May; Malcolm McIntyre and Alison Pendree (Champagne Bureau, London); Margery McKean; Jill Niblock (Flour Advisory Bureau); Belinda O'Hanlon (AnnaBelinda); Marsha Palanci and Jan Vachule (Schieffelin & Co.); Hilary Wharton. The drawings are by Linda Sandey.

Chapter One
BEFOREHAND

Engagement

Engagements are still formally announced through newspapers, both national and local. In some countries, such as Britain, a standard short announcement is used, on the lines of:

**Mr B. J. Rudge
and Miss M. A. Smith**

The engagement is announced between Barnaby, only son of Mr and Mrs David Rudge of Cheltenham and Mary, eldest daughter of Mr and Mrs John Smith of Cirencester.

Note: it is quite in order to replace 'Miss' by 'Ms', or even omit any title and refer to Mr B. J. Rudge and Mary Smith.

In the United States, more elaborate details are published, often together with a formal portrait of the woman. Give details of education and work experience and any other interesting points.

The bride's parents—or the bride—should send the announcement to the editor of the chosen paper several days beforehand. Make sure you say which day you want the announcement to appear, and include a daytime telephone number as the paper may well wish to check that the announcement is genuine.

Think about how much of your address you want to give. The more exact it is, the more likely you are to be inundated with circulars from wedding caterers, insurance agents, etc.

I asked Allison Guertin, herself newly engaged, how she announced her engagement:

I do think it is a good idea to announce your intentions to your parents as soon as possible. Do not do this over the telephone. Try to arrive with champagne in hand and surprise them with the good news and then toast the occasion together. If your parents are too far away to visit, try to send them a bottle, and telephone too, so that they know that, although far away, they are included in the celebration.

Allison suggests telling other people in a creative way.

One couple gathered their friends for opening day at the football stadium and had their message printed on the lighted scoreboard. Use family picnics, special events or college or school reunions where your friends are sure to attend. Do not announce your engagement at someone else's wedding, as you don't want to overshadow *their* special day.

The executive woman might well not tell anyone at work of her engagement (see page 76). Alternatively, she might prefer to announce it via the company newsletter or bulletin board. The future groom might similarly want to keep his engagement a secret—either to avoid embarrassment or simply because he does not think his private life is any concern of his colleagues'.

Start Thinking Now

It takes much longer to plan most weddings than you would imagine. When Dulcie House was helping organize her son's wedding she found that three months was barely enough time. 'They had been engaged nine months but suddenly a house came up. It was really a rush to get everything done in time.'

Once they had decided on a date, Dulcie's son and his fiancée set about organization in this order:

Date
Where and what time to be married
Where and when to have the reception

In this instance both bride and groom lived in the country and it was likely there would be conflict over availability of dates either for the church or reception. Details then followed (as they do in the order of this book).

It is never too soon to start planning. Some hotels have receptions booked three years ahead!

Bridesmaids

If the bride's sister is a bridesmaid or matron-of-honour (married attendant), ask someone from the groom's side too. Remember that all eyes are on the bride on the day, so it does not matter if the attendants are not Miss Worlds. Very young attendants may look cute, but they can distract attention and be too young to help.

Think About the Following

1. What you will wear (see pages 34-42).
2. What others will wear.
3. Your groom must think about his best man and ushers.
4. Who will give the reception (see page 12).
5. Where it will be (see pages 17-18).
6. Whether you need a marquee (large tent); you may have to reserve it literally months in advance.
7. How many people you will have (start making a guest list—and remember that your groom and both sets of parents will have lists too).
8. Think about a cake (see pages 24-7) and speeches (see pages 30-31).
9. Remember to book photographer (see pages 51-3) and transport (see page 54).
10. Remember to think about: hairdresser (beauty parlour)—(see page 42), rings (see pages 49-50), medical check-ups and passports (see page 74).
11. What about presents? (See pages 54-8).
12. Think about your going-away outfit.
13. What about a honeymoon? (See pages 31-4).

Note: the future groom will also have to start planning, although to a lesser extent. This book is essentially for the bride, but the groom, too, will find many worthwhile points in the ideas above.

Finance

A wedding can be an extremely costly affair. It is important to decide beforehand whether you want to work within a budget, or to 'throw caution to the winds and hang the cost'.

Ivor Spencer is often called in to organize a wedding.

> I advise people how to keep the costs down. They can close the bar early, they can serve inferior drink or, alternatively, serve real champagne but have a small number of guests. One subtle point of economy is to make sure the bride and groom leave early. As long as they are around everyone will go on drinking and this is how the overall costs can go up unbelievably.

Another way to cut costs is to separate the main reception (traditionally given by the bride's parents) from a general party. Some people, for instance, choose to have a reception and then a 'rest and tidy-up period' before a disco, in another place, at which it is quite obvious that everyone pays for their own drinks.

Who Pays for What?

The *reception* used to be the sole responsibility of the bride's parents, but now, increasingly, the groom's parents contribute, or even undertake the whole cost. Sometimes the bride and groom pay for their own reception. Every set of circumstances is different.

Traditionally, the *bride's parents* pay for:

1 Newspaper announcements.
2 The bride's dress (and perhaps at least a share of the bridesmaids').
3 Wedding invitations.
4 Flowers (though bouquets and buttonholes may be paid for by the best man).
5 Photographer/video.
6 Transport of the bridal party to church and reception.

The *groom* is responsible for:

1 Hiring his own clothes (and perhaps contributing to the cost for the ushers).
2 Church fees (other than flowers).
3 Rings.

4 Perhaps all bouquets and buttonholes.
5 Presents for the bridesmaids and, perhaps, for the ushers.

The bridesmaids (or their mothers) will probably have to contribute toward their outfits, nowadays. Depending on how great is their share, attendants should accordingly have a say in the choice of attire.

The *ushers* will probably have to pay at least in part for the hire of their clothes.

Service or Ceremony

If you intend to have a church wedding you should visit your minister as soon as possible. He will instruct you about procedures, including the publishing of banns (announcements publicly given during a church service). If you do not want the banns read, you can apply for an ecclesiastical licence. Ask your minister.

You may be able to be married on the day of your choice, but at some times of year there may well be a 'waiting list'. Services may also have to be held during certain hours, and legally the door must be open.

Note: remember to ask your minister his views about:

Music
Taping the ceremony
Photographs (see pages 52-3)
Confetti

It might be a good idea, too, to see if there are other services on the same day, so that you could share flowers for decorating the church.

Music

Talk to your minister beforehand to find out his views on music. If you are being married in a church he may feel strongly about, say, a modern rock band.

If there is a choir, ensure that it is strong enough to sing your choice of hymns. If there is no choir, choose hymns that most will know, and practise beforehand.

Make sure the musicians can cope—and check that the

instruments can cope, too, as even the most skilled organist may have problems with an unfamiliar, out-of-tune instrument.

Consider the length of the aisle. There is no point in choosing a short piece of music if you have to walk fifty yards in silence after it is over. If, on the other hand, your choice of music is too long, time the start of your progress accordingly.

Here are some much-loved wedding pieces:

Entrance of the Bride
Bliss—'A Wedding Fanfare'
Handel—'Arrival of the Queen of Sheba'
Mozart—'Wedding March' from *The Marriage of Figaro*
Purcell—'Fanfare'

Signing of the Register
Bach—'Air on the G String' (Aria from Suite in D)
   —'Ave Maria'
   —'Jesu, Joy of Man's Desiring'
Saint-Saens—'Benediction nuptiale'

Exit of Bride and Groom
Elgar—'Pomp and Circumstance March No. 4'
Hollins—'Bridal March'
Mendelssohn—'Wedding March' from *A Midsummer Night's Dream*
Wagner—'Wedding March' from *Lohengrin*

Note: music played at weddings is considered 'private', and is exempt from copyright fees.

Civil Ceremony

Divorced people and those not sharing the same religious beliefs are among those who may decide to marry in a civil ceremony. You should talk to your local registrar or Advice Bureau about it as soon as possible. It may be that certain residential qualifications are necessary to be married in the place of your choice—in Britain, for instance, marriage by licence requires that the bride or groom be resident for five clear days before marriage.

Remember, too, that register offices and other civil wedding venues may get booked up months ahead for Saturday mornings and other peak times.

You should ask:

1 What residential qualifications are necessary.
2 What legal papers are required.
3 How much the ceremony will cost.
4 How long it will last (so that you can time the reception).
5 What the ceremony consists of.
6 How many witnesses are required.
7 How many guests you are allowed.

Register Office

The wedding party should arrive about 10 minutes before the ceremony is due to start. (No-one should arrive more than 15 minutes beforehand or confusion is likely to occur with earlier parties). The attendant registrar will guide bride and groom through the order of ceremony. The register office ceremony will last about 10 minutes (confetti may not be allowed). Afterwards, there may be a full-scale reception.

Dress is less formal than for most church weddings. Brides often wear 'best dresses' or early cocktail attire, and carry a small bouquet. There are no bridesmaids as such.

Because usually so few guests can be admitted to a civil ceremony, invitations to those others invited to the reception following must be carefully worded. Similarly, if you want to tell friends about a civil ceremony that has already taken place, a simple wedding announcement may suffice (see page 47).

Blessing

A church blessing usually follows a wedding, perhaps one which has taken place in another country, or a local civil ceremony. There is no formal service as such,

usually prayers and an address. You should talk to the minister as far ahead as possible to see what he suggests, and what his ruling is on guests, flowers and music.

Reception

Still sometimes called the 'wedding breakfast', the reception following a marriage can cause many headaches and a good deal of expense.

Once you know the date and place of the wedding, start thinking about *where and when* the reception will be.

One advantage of having the reception in a hotel or hall is that much of the organization is done for you. The food and, perhaps, the drink and cake, will be taken care of. You therefore know exactly how much it will all cost. Your own home will also not be disrupted.

As soon as you can, look at several possible venues. Most can only do one or two weddings a day, and they may be booked up many months ahead. Visit as many as you can. Ask what their facilities are, and check prices. Do not be afraid to tell them your budget. Talk to anyone who has held a function there. If they are doing the catering, ask for a trial run of the menu.

As soon as you have made up your mind, make a definite booking. You should consider these points:

1 Remember how many people you told the hotel you would be having and stick to that number.
2 Will they be providing drink? If not, make other arrangements,
3 Will they be doing the cake? If not, make other arrangements (see pages 24-7).
4 Do you want music? If so, discuss it with the hotel and make suitable arrangements.
5 Remember that you need somewhere to change.
6 Check car-parking arrangements and the logistics of getting from church to reception.

If you decide to have your reception somewhere else you may well have to put more effort into the organization. If you decide to have the reception at home, consider these points:

1 Is the house big enough to cope?
2 If you want a marquee (tent) in the garden, is there room for it? Is there ample access from the house?
3 Can lavatory facilities cope?
4 Can car-park facilities cope?
5 Can you — and your parents — cope?

If you decide that it *is* possible to have the reception at home, as soon as you can:

1 Think about catering (see pages 19-23, 27-30).
2 Contact marquee suppliers (where relevant). Ask someone to come and look at the site.
3 If you want music, make suitable arrangements.
4 Think about the cake (see pages 24-7).

At some stage you should also consider the speeches (see pages 30-1).

Note: other ideas for receptions include:

1 Rent a bus and take everyone from the church/ ceremony to a distant eaterie like a fish and chip bar that you have pre-booked for several hours.
2 Rent a boat.
3 Borrow your local school hall (at least lavatory and car-park facilities should be adequate, though the ambience might not be superb).

Now think about *when*. If your reception is to follow the ceremony immediately, you are obviously governed by that timing. If the situation is more flexible, consider these points:

1 How far will guests have to travel?
2 How far will bride and groom have to travel afterwards?
3 When are the facilities available? Many restaurants, for instance, are delighted to cater for a group in between lunch and dinner sessions, say from around 3 p.m. onwards.

Food

If you are to be responsible for providing food and wine, you have first to decide *whether or not you want a caterer*. Some people find the convenience of having someone do all the food well worth while; others prefer to do it all themselves, not only because they think it works out less expensively but, as one person told me, 'I know what the guests will eat!'.

Be that as it may, the standard and price of function and contract caterers varies enormously. Try to select from personal recommendation or from experience. As in a hotel, ask for a trial run of the menu. If you do not like it, change it. Caterers should be helpful and interested in providing a high standard of service—if they are not, go elsewhere.

Sometimes the best caterers are those used to 'mass service'. In New Zealand, for instance, people often use racecourse caterers—Ellerslie Racecourse Receptions (Auckland) and Smith & Walding (Trentham Racecourse).

On the other hand, you may decide to do the catering yourself. Jane Howard, now Director of the Catering Market Division of Kingsway Public Relations, was working as a catering manager when she married. 'I thought, felt, ate and slept the daily crises and joys of large-scale catering. I wanted two things from my own reception. The food must be excellent and this must be achieved with the minimum of trouble'.

Here are some of Jane's ideas on wedding catering.

1 Make a list of equipment, both things *in situ* and things you can borrow (e.g. boiling rings, coffee percolators).
2 Write down the amount of available space for:
   (a) preparation (work surfaces);
   (b) primary cooking (ovens, grills);
   (c) holding/service (cupboards, shelves);
   (d) clearing up (sinks, spaces).
3 You can now tell whether or not you can plan a hot

meal (e.g. you have two large ovens and plenty of hot-cupboard space).

4 Now that you can also see where your congestion points are likely to be:

    (a) remember preparation space can be used during the reception for clearing;

    (b) check that you have enough holding/service space;

    (c) check that your clearing space can easily be cleared (if not, use high-quality disposable plates and cutlery).

The key is to plan the menu to suit the facilities available. Remember that cold starters and desserts can be pre-prepared and that generally buffets are more labour-intensive to prepare than entrées.

Note: whether you plan a fixed table d'hote or a buffet with choices, tell your guests what the menu is and how it is to be served (perhaps put standing cards on each table). If they know the procedure they will help you make the whole operation run more smoothly.

Service

The menu will suggest how food should be served. At some point, all dishes need portioning, which can be part of the cooking or the service. The simpler the food is to prepare—for example roast beef or poached salmon—the more complex it may be to serve, and vice versa.

It may be simplest to hire waiters and waitresses through a catering job bureau or catering school—or ask the banqueting manager of your favourite large hotel. Most 'ducks' (as they are called in the trade) work part-time for set hourly rates and provide their own uniform (often simple black and white). 1:20 is a reasonable ratio of skilled staff to guests; 1:15 for unskilled.

Arrange to meet your staff a few days before and give them a written brief on numbers attending, timing, dishes involved and how you want each served—i.e. to each person, or left centre-table for self-service. On the day, give them somewhere to change and a drink before they start. If you are going to tip (always a good idea) give this first: do not leave it until the reception is over or their good will won't be of any practical use. Ensure you adequately staff the kitchen area with professionals (or willing friends and relations) so that there will be no delay in the service.

Seated meals

If you have a seated meal, you may prefer to allow those other than the 'top table' to sit where they like. This is often preferable to trying to plan beforehand, as, invariably, some guests cannot make it at the last moment.

The main bridal party usually has seating arranged along one side of a table facing the guests. This gives as many people as possible a chance to see the bride and groom.

Typical seating is:

	Best man
	Bridesmaid
	Groom's father
T	Bride's mother
A	
B	Groom
L	
E	Bride
	Bride's father
	Groom's mother
	Usher
	Chief bridesmaid

It is a good idea to keep the food at a seated meal as simple as possible. If you want more elaborate food, go for a buffet.

Serve the foods 'plated', i.e. already portioned on to individual plates. All the guests will be in 'best clothes'

and many may be in hats, which makes serving from behind them difficult. The less that has to be 'passed through', the less likely it is that someone will have ice cream with raspberry sauce down her back.

Do not give too many choices of drinks. You will find, incidentally, that guests tend to drink more if they are seated (they have somewhere to put their glasses).

Pacing of the meal is important. Do not draw out the whole meal for too long: some of the guests may have to leave early.

Buffet Strategy
It is probably best to hire professional staff if you have something that is tricky to serve, say a dressed salmon or joint of beef. Do not waste money hiring a server for individually portioned dishes. If you do have a buffet server, the same points about staff briefing apply. Have adequate staff for clearing the used settings.

The traffic flow for buffets is vital. This is ideal:

T A B L E	Plates
	Salads and accompaniments
	Fish
	Meats
	Vegetables/(salads and accompaniments)
	Desserts

Bread, cutlery and condiments should go at the end or on tables.

This pattern can be repeated to give two or more service points, thus speeding up traffic accordingly. Remember that if guests have had to wait to pass the reception line on arriving at the reception they do not want to have to wait for food. To save hassle, you might consider placing the starters directly on the tables so that guests can immediately sit down and thereby avoid one session of queuing.

Wedding Brunch

If you really want to be traditional, try the wedding breakfast idea, translated as today's brunch, which means that you can serve a lighter, and therefore less costly, meal up to about 4 p.m. Streamline your menu and help your budget even further by simply serving eggs benedict (make them luxurious by replacing hollandaise with champagne and gruyère cheese), or make a large risotto.

The Cake

The cake occupies pride of place at the reception and the first slice is ceremoniously cut by the bride and groom. The cake is then removed and professionally cut behind the scenes. Small slices are handed round to all guests, either on plates or, ideally, on paper napkins, so that anyone who does not want to eat a slice can wrap it up and take it away.

Note: remember a cake knife!

Often the cake is tiered, with cakes of diminishing size one on top of the other. The bottom cake is cut, and a top layer may be kept for future use, say at a christening.

Nicky Roberts, Bakery Buyer for Harrods, told me that increasingly brides choose cake colours to match the whole wedding décor. A pale-blue Wedgwood-style cake with white decorations matches a 'pale-blue' wedding; a pale-pink cake with roses will complement a bride with a pale-pink rose bouquet, and so on. She finds today that many like cream-coloured icings.

In many parts of the world, a rich dark fruit cake is used, often still made at home according to a long-passed-down recipe. It should be made at least a week in advance and then covered with almond paste (marzipan), which is available commercially although many *aficionados* claim that whereas you can save time by buying in a cake, you should always use home-made almond paste.

If you want a copy of recipes for wedding cake and almond paste, together with instructions for royal icing, specially provided by the Flour Advisory Bureau, contact them at 21 Arlington Street, London SW1A 1RN.

Such a fruit cake is then covered with royal icing, composed of finely sieved icing sugar, egg whites and glycerine. Icing is the trickiest part of cake-making

and, also, it is the part that shows. You may well decide that this is the stage that should be handed over to a professional. The trouble is that few professionals will ice someone else's cake, so *before you start baking check that you have someone to do the icing!*

If you decide to do the icing yourself, why not simplify the process? You could deliberately form the surface into an uneven terrain of bumps, like a 'snow-terrain' Christmas cake, and you can also buy cake decorations.

In other parts of the world, such as the USA, a light 'white cake' is preferred, perhaps a fatless sponge or a Victoria sponge. The icing may then be a soft butter cream or a commercial frosting, and perhaps decorated with flowers.

When President Reagan's daughter Patti Davis got married, for instance, she had a four-tiered white cake with lemon cream filling, decorated with gardenias, lilies and white stephanotis (and the reception, at the Bel Air in Los Angeles, included a menu of green salad, grilled chicken with rosemary, baby vegetables and Californian sparkling wine).

If you are invited to a wedding in *Finland*, you will also find a white cake, but each layer may have a filling of fresh strawberries and cream. By contrast, a cake in *Germany* consists of lower layers of biscuit and butter-cream sandwich.

Other ideas for an alternative to the 'ordinary fruit cake' include Harrods' profiterole towers (with toffee icing). And Nicky Roberts told me of one bride who wanted a cake cut and decorated like a bed, complete with miniature couple!

Whatever type of cake you decide to have, remember to consider its shape. There is no point in choosing a five-tiered cake if you are only five feet tall. Remember that a tall cake looks better in a tall room.

Note: do pick the cake up from the baker in plenty of time. The weight of a fruit cake should make it fairly easy to transport from baker to reception, but the slightest jolt, say at a traffic light, might damage the decoration. Lace-work is especially vulnerable. Bakers have often had to work through the night to repair damage: try to pick the cake up at least a week before the wedding just in case anything goes wrong.

To keep tiers of fruit cake simply wrap them in tissue paper and put in an airtight tin. Because fruit gradually seeps through, the icing will discolour, but many firms will re-ice any cake they originally baked and iced.

Champagne

At the wedding breakfast of the Prince and Princess of Wales, 29 July 1981, Krug Collection 1969 was served. This champagne, in magnum, is made from twenty-four different growths with the following grape proportions:

Pinot Noir 45%
Chardonnay 34%
Meunier 21%

Champagne is the traditional wedding drink. It is, alas, extremely costly.

How Much per Person?
If you are serving champagne throughout, allow half a bottle per person. If you are offering champagne only for the toast, calculate a bottle to six people.

Bottle sizes
Quarter-bottle (split)	187 ml
Half-bottle	375 ml
Standard bottle	750 ml
Magnum (2 bottles)	1.5 l
Jeroboam (4 bottles)	3 l
Methusalem (8 bottles)	6 l
Salmanazar (12 bottles)	9 l

Serving
Many caterers prefer to pour from ordinary-sized bottles, as they are easier to handle. If you are serving, however, you may like to use magnums, which certainly look more spectacular.

Champagne should never be served ice-cold as over-chilling masks the delicate bouquet. Ideal bottle temperature is 42-48°F. If you have a small number of guests, achieve the correct temperature by merely putting the bottle for 30 minutes in an ice bucket (or plastic bucket) half-filled with a mixture of ice and water. If you have more guests, you may want to use large plastic containers, such as (clean!) dustbins, filled with water and ice.

Use slender glass flutes or tulip-shaped glasses. Some *cognoscenti* use a narrow rounded flute with a slight waist towards the top to retain the bouquet. Do not use flat 'coupes', which should be reserved for ice-cream sundaes.

A champagne bottle contains up to 90 pounds of pressure per square inch, so open it carefully. Unwind and remove the wire muzzle. Grasp the cork in one hand and the bottle in the other, at an angle of 45

degrees away from you and everyone else. Slowly twist the bottle—not the cork. When the cork is out, keep the bottle at a 45-degree angle for a few seconds to allow surplus gas to escape.

Ideally, you should pour champagne holding the bottle by the bottom indentation (the punt). Pour about an inch into each glass, and then half-fill.

Many sparkling wines are also excellent. I am particularly fond of some Spanish *cavas* and such Californian 'champagnes' as those produced by Chateau St Jean, Domaine Chandon, Hanns Kornell and Schramsberg. Richard Furnival Jones, in Harrods' wine department, suggests a sparkling Saumur.

To make your wedding really memorable, how about trying a champagne pyramid?

Nancy Jarratt told me about Moët & Chandon's famous *cascade*: a pyramid of handmade crystal glasses. Many glasses are set side by side on an absolutely flat surface, with fewer and still fewer glasses on top. The idea is to see how tall a pyramid you can create (Nancy says she has seen one with 1,365 glasses).

Champagne is carefully poured into the top glass. When this is filled, the champagne overflows into those beneath, and so on down. (One of my 'drinks' friends told me he did this recently in his department but, alas, a small mischief maker pulled out one of the bottom glasses, which ruined the pyramid and resulted in a lot of broken glass!).

Ideally, a *cascade* should be filled by *sabrage* (the name comes from the traditional French cavalry officer's sabre, which was used swiftly to slice the neck off a bottle).

Other Wines

If you serve only one wine, make it white and not too sweet. Richard Furnival Jones suggests:

Muscadet
Any Loire wine

Any Alsace wine
A German Rhine or (probably a bit sweeter) Moselle.

As with champagne, make sure the wine is adequately chilled and serve it in the nicest glasses you can.

Non-Alcoholic Drinks

You should always have alternatives for those who do not want alcohol and, bearing in mind that some may have to drive long distances afterwards, it is good to have water, soft drinks and/or tea and coffee available.

Remember to offer a choice of non-alcoholic drinks—not just thick tomato juice! Have a clean light drink (such as apple juice) available for those who prefer it, and for young children.

Speeches

In the West, speeches at the reception are generally made in the following order:

1 An old friend of the bride (or her father) proposes the health of the bride and groom.
2 The groom responds, thanking the bride's parents, his parents and anyone else appropriate, and proposes a toast to the bridesmaids.
3 The best man replies on the bridesmaids' behalf and, at this point, may read out any sent-in messages.

Ivor Spencer tells of some embarrassing moments at weddings he has been to. 'There was the bridegroom who started his speech "Thank you for coming to this memorial occasion",' he told me, 'and there was a photographer who unwittingly told the bride's mother that "Grandmothers are not in this particular picture, ma'am".'

If you are to make a speech:

1 Do avoid embarrassing reminiscences of the bride as a small child wetting her pants. And if you are going to make jokes, try them out first on a close relative. Judge by their reaction as to whether or not you can tell the story in public.

2 Be as brief as possible. It is a good idea for everyone to be set a time limit (say two minutes). It may be that all the guests are standing and their feet hurt. It may also happen that none of the speakers is proficient and/or confident.

3 Unless you are very experienced, plan beforehand what you are going to say.

4 Do your homework, so that you do not make any embarrassing gaffes.

5 Make notes, or at least prominent headings, written fairly large so that you can see them clearly. If you use more than one sheet of paper or notecard, number each leaf.

6 Dress unobtrusively. Try to avoid anything that jangles.

7 Do not drink too much.

8 Before you start, take a deep breath. Stand comfortably, your feet slightly apart. Have something to hold in your hands or, if this is impossible, hold your hands together behind your back.

9 Speak slowly and clearly. Look at the audience and try to speak to everyone: do not stare without interruption at one person.

10 Vary your speed of talking and your voice level.

Note: if you want to add some extra liveliness to your reception, why not follow the Hungarian custom whereby every guest tries to dance—one at a time—with the bride, in return for a 'contribution' of money, put into a handy receptacle? The income might even pay for the whole reception!

Honeymoon

A honeymoon is important. Traditionally it is held immediately after the wedding, but increasingly today the bride and groom prefer a holiday either before the wedding ('to get in form') or some time afterwards when all the activity has subsided.

Regardless of your budget, it is a good idea to have a change from what will later be your normal routine. If you are putting all your money into your new house, why not simply tell everyone you are going away and then slip away to your new house? Make sure you have ample food and drink in store, take the telephone off the hook—and have the holiday of a lifetime.

If you do decide to go away immediately after the wedding reception, try to avoid too much travel on the first night. Many a couple has had the reception ruined by worrying about a long drive to the airport. It may be a good idea to spend the first night in a convenient good hotel and fly to your destination the following morning.

I have been married (to the same man!) for nearly twenty years and we spent our honeymoon variously camping in Wales, Ireland and Scotland and on a Russian ship in the Eastern Mediterranean.

Were I asked today, I think I would choose a short stay in a luxury venue (that is to say, one night at a Savoy-style hotel rather than six in a converted brothel in Zanzibar). My luxurious honeymoon suggestions would include these hotels, all chosen because:

1 They are small.
2 They have intimate restaurants.
3 There are good things to do locally (shopping, walking).
4 Bedrooms are attractive and well-appointed.

Bath—Ston Easton Georgian mansion, large country estate.

Derbyshire—Peacock at Rowsley Elizabethan manor in a tiny village.

Houston—La Colombe D'Or Near to the Galleria shopping.

Kashmir—Harmukh Houseboat. Idyllic calm (and Mick Jagger stayed here!).

London—Stafford Real Christmas trees in your room.

New Forest—Chewton Glen Local countryside—good food.

BEFOREHAND

Oxfordshire—Le Manoir aux Quat'Saisons Stunning décor—old manor, good food.

Sonoma Valley—Sonoma Mission Inn Magnificent sports facilities—and a spa to help you feel fit.

St Paul de Vence—La Colombe D'Or The original, from which the Texan one took inspiration. Full of priceless French paintings, with all the life of the South of France around.

Venice—Sheraton Grand Hotel Orologio Forty-five minutes' drive west, in the spa resort of Abano Terme, this hotel has magnificent gardens, spacious rooms, absolute quiet and super food, as well as healthy spa treatments!

If you prefer larger hotels, however, here are some with special honeymoon appeal, and 'all-found' packages:

Gloucester Country Club Outstanding sports facilities.

Macau—Hyatt Regency This modern hotel consists of units constructed and shipped as containers from Alabama, and combines Portuguese relaxation with the fascination of Macau.

Note: if you fly with some airlines (Gulf Air, for example), they will give you a special honeymoon cake, provided you tell them beforehand!

The Bride

Fitness and Beauty
You want to look your best. If you are not already eating well, start your 'wedding eating plan' well before the wedding.

Your skin needs to look sparkling. Make sure you get plenty of Vitamin A (dairy produce, green vegetables, offal), potassium (have a banana a day) and zinc (eat seafood). Healthy hair comes from Vitamin A and Vitamin B_2 (yoghurt, eggs, liver) and zinc. If your nails are bad, concentrate on calcium (dairy produce and wholewheat bread). You cannot afford to feel run down and suffer from intestinal problems; you need iron and folic acid in the form of green vegetables, nuts, meat, and dairy produce.

Fitness is really important. It is not that a bride needs necessarily to diet for the Big Day, but she should be feeling her best, and this means getting into shape in plenty of time.

Here are some special bride-to-be exercises conceived by Strong, Stretched and Centered, based on Maui—the Hawaiian island that I always associate with sparkling health and vitality. (Can you imagine anything more elevating than exercising right by the water's edge, with brightly coloured Hawaiian flowers all around and a clear blue sky above?)

(Remember to *warm up* first—shake your arms, shake your legs, and stretch up as far as you can.)

Sparkle Stretch   This stretch strengthens and limbers the entire back, with emphasis on the lower back. It also stretches out the back of your legs, tones the calves and builds strong arches. And, in addition, it firms up the tummy muscles, elongates the spine, opens up the chest and lifts the shoulders—really giving you a sparkle!

This is what you do:

1 Stand with your feet apart, parallel on the outside edge. Arms are extended straight out sideways from the shoulders. Relax the knees slightly and drop the pelvis forward just enough so that the rib cage is directly over your hips (this will take all the sway out of the lower back). Keep your chin level, thus keeping the vertebrae in your neck long.

2 Inhale and start bending forward from the waist, taking care to keep your back flat and fully extended. Let your arms cross gracefully in front of you so that when your back is parallel to the floor your arms are fully crossed.

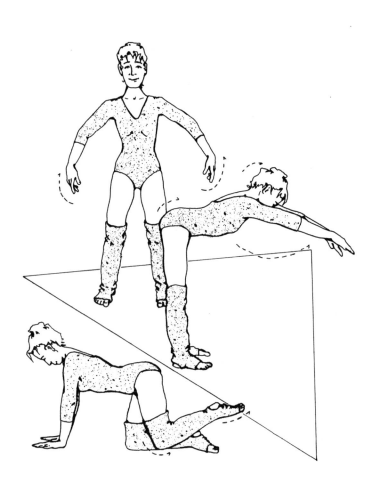

3 Exhale as you lift your body, keeping your arms crossed over your head.
4 When your body is upright, uncross your arms to the first fully extended position.

Firm kick This tones your legs and buttocks, strengthens the tummy muscles and firms the waistline.

1 Kneel on all fours. Now bring one leg straight out from the hip parallel to the floor (leg should be bent at the knee with the foot in point) and place the opposite hand on the hip. Your chest must remain open throughout this entire exercise. Keep your tummy muscles contracted and the leg lifted and do not ever let the moving leg drop below hip level.
2 Straighten and bend the lifted knee. Do this 20 times, foot in point. Repeat with the foot flexed. Do the other side. Now back to the first side with a count of 15. Repeat through a count of ten and finally a count of five.

Professional help
Nothing is nicer than a 'complete health treatment' just prior to the wedding, say the day before.

I talked to Kay Harding at Harrods and she told me about their special programmes. 'Our Top To Toe programme lasts nearly five hours. It includes a sauna, body massage, manicure and pedicure, facial, shampoo, and blow-dry or set. It is perfect for brides—and for their mothers. We also do a Total Look programme, which lasts about six hours and has additional hair cut and such details as eyebrow trim.

With such professional help, the bride should feel her very best.

The Dress
Sarah Appleby at Harrods says that even the most sophisticated woman often becomes quite demure when choosing her wedding dress. This is the one time in her life when she adheres to tradition.

Ideally, Sarah Appleby likes her customers to come in

as early as six months before the wedding. It may take time to choose a dress and then there are the required fittings.

The advantage, incidentally, of going to a department store is that the whole look can be co-ordinated. Veil or headdress, underclothes and shoes can be chosen to complement the dress, and all can be packed up together in a large 'trousseau box' so that the bride knows she has everything she needs for the wedding.

Most brides come to choosing their dress 'completely fresh'. They have never done it before! Contrary to supposition, most wedding dresses look best on a curved size 12 (British: American 10, Continental 40). Model figures are more difficult to accommodate.

It does not matter what shape you are. Go for proportion. If you are big-busted, avoid a high neckline; go for something which shows your neck to advantage. Short women should avoid too many obvious horizontal lines (rows of frills), and tall brides may want to avoid vertical stripes.

Go for something which you feel good in. Ask the advice of the people in the shop. They work with wedding dresses every day, and they are there to help you.

You may be looking for a dress which you can use again, but people in the trade say that this seldom happens. In my own case, I had lots of good intentions of shortening my dress and wearing it again, but it looked like a sack of potatoes when short and I threw it away.

Remember that the back of your gown will be seen as you walk up, and then, later, down the aisle, and also at your reception. If you are travelling to the service in a small car or carriage, it is probably best to avoid a long train (remember the Princess of Wales's problems in trying to extricate her long train on arrival at St Paul's Cathedral?).

Make sure that when you try on your dress you wear the underclothes that you will wear on 'the day'. Look at how the dress suits you in artificial light as well as daylight.

If you are a winter bride, be realistic and do not go for too low a neckline. Today the modern bride can wear something sensible to beat possible cold : in the 1984 winter collections, for instance, Karl Lagerfeld for Chanel showed a demurely high-collared long slim white wool coat with a gold chain wreathing the waist and gold buttons all down the front.

Of course, you may go for sheer originality. I heard not long ago of a bride who had chosen a red-and-black dress with a black hat—and I saw a letter in the *Los Angeles Times* not long ago in which a future bride asked for advice on a wedding jumpsuit. One of the forthcoming suggestions was a white satin jumpsuit with removable full-length white lace skirt!

Dress hire   If you decide to hire your dress, make sure it arrives in plenty of time. It is always good to have 'time in hand'.

Dress makers   If you decide to make your dress, start sewing well ahead of time, as there is invariably an unexpected escalation of pre-wedding activity as the date itself draws nearer. Do not be discouraged if you get a tiny spot on the garment: if it is small enough it will not show on the day.

As well as the dress, you will need:

Veil or headcover
Suitable underclothes
Stockings or tights
Shoes

Traditionally, the bride's veil is thrown back after the ceremony, revealing her face.

Old lace veils are heavy to wear and are best held in place by a heavy tiara. Alice bands or circlets can be

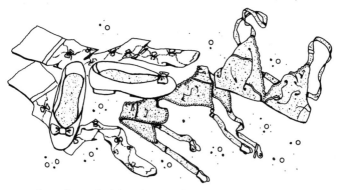

employed to hold other types of veil. Silk net is expensive, but it is light to wear and easy to hold in place. Nylon net, the least expensive, is slippery and difficult to keep in place.

Take along a sample of your dress fabric when going to choose the veil, so that it will exactly match or complement it.

To attach a veil, place an alice band or circlet on the head of the 'bride'. Position the veil over it. If you are working with an alice band, sew the veil in place to the back of the band. If you are working with a circlet, sew it to the back of the circlet. You will now see that the front of the veil can be pulled back, doubled over at the stitchings, to reveal the face.

Instead of a veil, you may prefer a hat. Make sure that it is securely fastened to your head.

Underclothes Sarah Appleby said that even women who do not generally wear bras may choose to do so on their wedding day, often to complement a dress that is traditionally a 'corseted style'.

This is one occasion, incidentally, when you do not want your bra showing through your dress—and you certainly do not want bra straps spoiling your neckline.

Try on your dress with the bra you will be wearing on the day. If a white bra shows through, try a natural-coloured one. If straps tend to show, sew little retainers to the inside of the dress shoulder seams (small loops of ribbon with popper studs).

Shoes and hosiery   Whatever happens, do not wear new shoes on the day. They may slip or rub. You may forget to take the price ticket off the bottom, and your 'special bargain' will be revealed as you kneel at the altar.

If you are marrying someone who was never meant to be a basketball star, do not wear your highest heels. Wear shoes that are suitable—and comfortable. No-one will look too closely at your feet.

On the other hand, they *will* notice if you wear too-dark stockings. If you are wearing a white dress, go for white or ultra-pale stockings or tights.

If you normally wear tights but have always longed for sexy stockings, this is not the occasion to experiment. Try that on your honeymoon!

Hair and make-up   It is essential for a bride to try her hairstyle beforehand. Many hairdressers suggest coming in, with headdress, about a week beforehand. If you are going to have a heavy veil or tiara it is well worth while having it professionally fixed.

Make-up artist Gerald told me that it is impossible for a bride to have her face professionally made-up the night before. 'You just have to come in early on the day,' he said.

He advises a natural make-up, plus photographic techniques such as making the eyes look bigger. Because there may be quite a lot of kissing of friends and relatives, it is a good idea to stabilize lipstick.

He tends to use soft cold colours for European brides—blues and violets, to make them look younger. Oriental brides can wear warmer make-up colours.

The Bridal Party
What the bride and groom and their attendants can and should wear is described on pages 12-15 and 37-42.

Other members of the bridal party (bride's and groom's parents, and other close relations) are also important, although not vital. You do not want Gloria's mother turning up in shocking pink and Horace's in orange stripes. Similarly, it is not a good idea for Gloria's mother and three aunts all to be wearing enormous hats with long veils, while Horace's mother and sisters are bare-headed and wearing open-toed sandals.

Sometimes mothers do not want anyone to know what they are going to wear. Others simply do not know themselves until the day before the wedding (Dulcie House was so busy for two weeks before her son's wedding, planning a sit-down meal for 120 people, that she had no idea what she was going to put on).

For the sake of the photographs, it really is a good idea to liaise at least as far as (*a*) colour and (*b*) formality are concerned.

Note: when you consider colour, bear in mind the colours of the church carpet and the flowers.

Regardless of what other men wear, traditionally the fathers of the bride and groom follow the groom's lead. If he wears formal attire, then so should they.

Guests

The inescapable fact here is that you cannot please everyone. If you have a guest list of ten, the person who would have been number 11 on your list is offended. If you plan a 'little wedding' with two thousand guests, you will *still* upset someone.

What is the answer? The bride and groom could always elope... but that is cheating.

Everyone has to be *firm*.

1 Whoever is giving the reception (say the bride's parents) must be firm, and tell the groom's parents—and the bride and groom—that there must be a limit of x on the total number of guests, and that therefore they can only invite y of those on the groom's parents' list.

2 The others submitting lists (groom's parents and bride and groom) must accept the fact that this is not an occasion for a free bonanza for everyone they ever knew or hoped they might have the chance to know.

3 Those who are invited should not gloat about it—and certainly should not publicly display their invitation if the wedding is a small affair.

4 Those not on the list should appreciate the difficulty the host has undoubtedly had in deciding who should go. There are many constraints on his choice—both sets of parents have family and long-time friends, quite apart from the friends of the bride and groom.

If you are not invited, it is still in order to go to the church but play a low-key role. You may also send a gift, if you wish, without embarrassment.

Note: if you are unable to ask all those you would like to the main reception, why not ask others to come to a 'cash bar' party, either some days before the wedding or after it?

Invitations

For all but the smallest weddings, traditionally invitations are engraved (preferably) or printed. The names of the guests are formally handwritten in the top left-hand corner:

Mr and Mrs Adolphus Milk

and, if a child is included:

Mr and Mrs Adolphus Milk and Daisy.

Invitations generally come from the bride's parents, indicating that they paid for the reception.

Typically, invitations read:

Mr and Mrs John Smith
request the pleasure of your company
at the marriage of their daughter
Mary Jane
to
Mr Wallaby Budge
at St George's Church, Havanhold
on Saturday, 20th July at 2.30 p.m.
and afterwards at Cozynook Manor, Forever

Mrs John Smith
25 Gay Lane
Newington NW12 1CB   RSVP

If the bride's parents are giving the wedding, it is customary for the groom's parents to provide a list of the people they would like to invite. It is a matter of mutual trust for the groom's family not to demand too many guests. It is customary for an invitation to be sent to the groom's parents, even though it may be obvious they will be there.

Realistically, today, other situations may arise:

1 If the reception is being given by the bride and groom, the invitation should read:

Wallaby Budge and Mary Jane Smith
request the pleasure of your company
at their marriage
at...

2 If the reception is given jointly by the parents of bride and groom, the invitation should read:

Mr and Mrs John Smith
and
Mr and Mrs Barnaby Budge
request the pleasure of your company
at the marriage of
Mary Jane
to
Mr Wallaby Budge
at...

3 If the bride's parents are divorced and are sharing the hospitality, the invitations should read:

> Mr John Smith and Mrs Jane Smith
> request the pleasure of your company
> at the marriage of their daughter…

4 If the bride's divorced mother has remarried and she and her husband are giving the wedding, the invitations should read:

> Mr and Mrs Harold Holdem
> request the pleasure of your company
> at the marriage of her daughter
> Mary Jane Smith
> to
> Mr Wallaby Budge
> at…

5 If the bride's divorced father has remarried and he and his wife are giving the wedding, the invitations should read:

> Mr and Mrs John Smith
> request the pleasure of your company
> at the marriage of his daughter
> Mary Jane
> to
> Mr Wallaby Budge
> at…

6 If the bride's parents are dead and someone else is giving the wedding and wishes to honour the parents, the invitations could read:

> Mr and Mrs Charles E. Craft II
> request the pleasure of your company at the marriage
> of
> Mary Jane
> daughter of the late Mr and Mrs John Smith
> to
> Mr Wallaby Budge
> at…

7 If a civil ceremony is to be held, invitations can be sent to all those invited to the following reception (the few who are to be present at the ceremony itself can be personally invited):

Mr and Mrs John Smith
request the pleasure of your company
following the marriage of their daughter
Mary Jane
to
Mr Wallaby Budge
on Saturday, 20 July at 3.00 p.m.
at Cozynook Manor, Forever

Mrs John Smith
25 Gay Lane
Newington NW12 1CB   RSVP

---

8 After a civil ceremony you may want to send out an announcement:

Mr and Mrs John Smith
announce with great pleasure
the marriage of their daughter
Mary Jane
to
Mr Wallaby Budge
on Saturday, 20th July

---

9 If a Service of Blessing is being held, invitations may read:

Mr and Mrs John Smith
request the pleasure of your company at
a Service of Blessing the marriage of their daughter
Mary Jane
to
Mr Wallaby Budge
at St George's Church, Havanhold
on Saturday, 20th July at 2.30 p.m.
and afterwards at Cozynook Manor, Forever

Mrs John Smith
25 Gay Lane
Newington NW12 1CB   RSVP

Note: if there is to be a dance after the wedding, this should be stated, with an indication of suitable dress, in the bottom right-hand corner of the invitation.

Flowers

When Prince Charles married Lady Diana Spencer in 1981, her bouquet was a gift from the Worshipful Company of Gardeners of London. Carrying on a family tradition, Mr David Longman of Longmans Ltd was asked to design and prepare the bouquet. (In 1947, his father was responsible for Her Majesty the Queen's bouquet.)

Lady Diana's bouquet was a shower design with graceful flowing lines. The centre was composed of gardenias supported by golden Mountbatten roses, to honour the memory of Lord Mountbatten, and there was a cascade of white Odontoglossum orchids. From this fell a shower of stephanotis supported by miniature ivy and tradescantia leaves. A spray of orchids rose from the centre, surrounded by lily-of-the-valley and white freesias. As is traditional in royal weddings, myrtle and veronica, both from bushes grown from sprigs in Queen Victoria's bouquet, were also included.

Flowers have special meanings attached to them. Here are some:

Camellia—gratitude
Forget-me-not—true love
Iris—hidden message
Lily—majesty (*white lily*—purity; *pink lily*—talent)
Lily-of-the-valley—happiness
Mimosa—sensitivity
Orange blossom—chastity
Rose—love
Snowdrop—hope
Sweet pea—pleasure
Violet—faithfulness

By contrast, flowers you might want to avoid at weddings include cyclamen (diffidence), hydrangeas (boastfulness), larkspur (fickleness), marigolds (grief)

and narcissus (egotism)!

I spoke to Ann Wardill, florist at Harrods. Ideally she likes a bride to come in as soon as she has chosen her dress. 'If she brings a sample of the fabric she can look through our books and make her choice.'

Bouquets should be freshly made, but if dampened, covered with moist tissue and kept cool (not in a fridge) they will stay fresh for many hours.

Ann has made up many unusual bouquets, including 'vegetable bouquets' with carrots, cabbage leaves and spring onions. Most often, however, she uses lilies, stephanotis and orchids.

Why not keep a memento of the wedding in the form of a pressed flower picture? When Helena Cobban married Bill Quandt in Washington DC not long ago, her page and bridesmaid, Tarek and Leila Rached, removed sprigs from the bouquet and placed them between sheets of tissue paper in a flower press. (If you do not have a press, put the tissue paper sandwich under sheets of ordinary newspaper and a heavy weight such as an iron or a pile of hardback books.) Later the pressed flowers can be made into a collage and framed.

Rings

Although some women wear engagement rings that have been handed down through the family, most have new wedding rings.

Whether or not the groom also has a wedding ring is a matter of personal choice and local custom.

When choosing the bride's wedding ring, remember to make sure that it 'goes' with her other jewellery, as well as with her engagement ring. It is a good idea to choose a ring that is, if anything, slightly too loose rather than too tight. Many young brides later acquire wifely spread, and fingers swell.

Note: make sure the wedding ring is kept really safely until the day! Do not lose it.

Wedding Superstitions

Here are some 'old wives' tales' (*not* believed at all by the author, of course, who got married on a Saturday!).

Days of the week

Monday brides will be healthy
Tuesday brides will be wealthy
Wednesday brides will do best of all
Thursday brides may be unlucky
Friday brides will suffer losses
Saturday brides will have no luck

Note: this is rather surprising, in view of the fact that most get married on a Saturday!

BEFOREHAND

Tying a shoe to the bridal car
A reminder that in olden days the father of the bride gave one of her shoes to the husband, so that he, as 'master', could tap her with it.

Colours for the bride's dress

White — suitable
Green — you may not be around for long
Red — most unlucky
Yellow — you are ashamed of your man
Brown — you may go to live away from town
Grey — you will travel a lot
Black — you are sad about the wedding
Pink — not good for future fortunes
Blue — your lover is true

And

1 A bride should not see her groom on the day of the wedding until they meet at the church/ceremony.
2 A groom should not see his future bride's dress before the wedding.
3 It is lucky for the bride to meet a black cat, lamb or spider on the way to the church, but unlucky to pass a pig or a funeral.
4 Then there's the first letter of your surname:

> Change the name and not the letter:
> You'll marry for worse and not for better.

5 Finally, the old favourite — the bride should wear:

> Something old, something new,
> Something borrowed, something blue.

Photographs or Video

Remember that you cannot recreate your wedding. If you ask Uncle Umberto to take the pictures and his shutter sticks — you have had it.

It is not a good idea in any case to ask a relation or even a close friend to take the photographs — unless you want to endanger future good relations. It is much better to invest in a professional photographer.

Professional photographers are experienced in getting ample pictures of all the important people. Once you have decided whom you will use, talk to the photographer and tell him what shots you want. Do you want pictures of the bride's arrival at church? Are photographs allowed inside the church? (Check with the vicar.) Where will the formal after-service pictures be taken? (If outside, consider contingency wet-weather plans.) Describe the place where the reception will be and, if possible, show the photographer so that lighting can be assessed.

Many brides like the idea of informal shots, perhaps showing the aforementioned uncle—relieved of the onerous task of having to take pictures—stuffing himself with wedding cake. If you want informal 'candids', tell the photographer. But do also have some formal 'posed shots' for your relations and for your own future perusal.

At the moment, video-recording a wedding is definitely best left to professionals. They know how to be as unobtrusive as possible and still produce a well-edited film that does not consist of drunken panning from one side of the reception room to the other.

Transport

Generally, the organizer of the wedding is responsible *only* for the following transport:

Getting to the church:

Bride's mother
Bridesmaids
Bride and father (or whoever is giving her away)

From church to reception:

Bride and groom
Attendants
Bride's parents
Groom's parents

From reception:

Bride and groom.

If you have guests coming a long way, say by train, it is courteous to provide them with some means of getting to the wedding. If enough people are coming on one train, it might be worth your while to ask a local coach company to lay on a bus. If you do not want to pay for it, contact all relevant guests and tell them that transport will be provided by 'X Company' at a cost of *y*.

Note: remember that it may rain. I was all set to walk to and from my wedding but we had enormous sheets of clear plastic ready, 'in case.'

Presents

First of all, it should be assumed by everyone that *the marriage is going to last.* Therefore even if you cannot believe that Araminta is going to put up with Archibald for more than a year, the gift you choose should not take that into account.

The *bride* must choose whether or not she wants to give some indication of what she would like, or whether she would prefer to leave it to her guests' discretion. Things she should bear in mind include the following:

1 Will she be in a new home after marriage?
2 Do she and the man she is going to marry already have 'all the essentials'?
3 Would they prefer to give guests an indication of what china and glass they would like?

If so, it is well worth her time going to a local store and choosing suitable designs.

If, as the future bride, you do choose to make a list, remember to include things as small as a tea-towel, as well as large expensive items. (To make sure you do not overlook anything your future household might need, look at some of the sample present lists published in most issues of bridal magazines.)

Some stores will keep *bride's lists* and make them available to any guest. The store can thus direct the guest to a suitable place setting, etc. Such stores have their own dummy lists to help guide you.

In view of the distances often involved, it might be more practical for the bride's mother to keep some xeroxed copies of the lists of china, cutlery (flatware) and other items wanted by the bride. Anyone asking for a copy of the list could then be sent it.

In Edinburgh, for instance, Debenham's bride's list is available from their Princes Street shop (telephone *031-225-1320)*. The list is broken down into the following categories:

China—everything from best dinner service to butter dish.
Cutlery—including carving set and everyday teaspoons.
Electrical appliances—ranging from 'essentials' like a kettle to such a 'luxury' as a video recorder.*
General—even ashtrays are needed, and this category also includes a magazine rack and bathroom scales.
Glass—from everyday tumblers to brandy glasses.
Kitchen—everything for the beginner through to the advanced cook.
Linen—all necessary bathroom, bedroom and table items.

Note: I am told that generally today a mere vacuum cleaner is 'too mundane' and often guests will choose designer-decorated toasters and kettles rather than plain ones.

For suggestions of what is needed for the average household, see brides' magazines or ask your local department store.

Procedure
Presents should ideally be sent in plenty of time before the wedding so that:

1 The bride can write her thank you notes before the wedding.
2 The gifts can be displayed on the day.

If presents are taken on the day, they should be handed to someone responsible at the reception. Each gift should have the card from the donor clearly displayed, and the donor's name and address should also be attached inside the box or parcel.

From the *guest's* point of view, it is always a good idea to find out if the bride has made a list. Ask her mother when replying to the invitation. If there is a list, you are not bound by it, but it may be some help.

If there is no list, ask yourself whether or not the bride would like a practical gift. Would an ironing board be appreciated — or have she and her fiancé had their own homes for so long that they already have two of such necessities and certainly do not want another? If you think a practical gift *is* the answer, a visit to any hardware or kitchen shop should produce several ideas within your price bracket.

Avoid giving one of a place setting that you — and not the bride — have chosen. This looks rather as though you are assuming that the bride will have to eat alone every night.

If practical gifts are not in order, here are some alternative ideas:

A really beautiful large ashtray
Wine
A decanter
A five-year subscription to a 'luxury' magazine
Honeypot and spoon
Hand towels
Seeds or a small plant for the garden.

Some people have developed their own 'special gift'. One headmaster was a valued guest at his former students' weddings, as he always produced a good set of carvers. Similarly, Ralph Taylor, General Manager of Maxim's in London, likes to send a bottle of champagne and two rather beautiful glasses as an 'extra' wedding present — 'for your honeymoon'.

When you have chosen your gift, adhere to custom. In Britain, for instance, it is very bad form to take your gift to the reception. It should be delivered or sent beforehand, preferably to the bride's home. She can reply to thank you as soon as it has been received. In the US, on the other hand, it is quite in order for the gift to be taken to the reception, elaborately wrapped and well labelled, and the bride has a year in which to reply.

Do make sure that your gift is well packaged. If you are sending china or glass it is a good idea to enclose a card saying where the purchase was made, in case there is any damage.

'Showers'

Smaller gifts are also offered to the bride at showers. Essentially an American phenomenon, these are normally women's parties, given by someone in honour of a bride-to-be. Supposing Nancy, soon to be married, has an aunt who wants to give a shower, say for ten people. Nancy will give her aunt the names and addresses of ten friends whom she would like invited — they do not have to be known to the host.

Showers usually have themes, say a 'kitchen shower' or an 'all-blue shower', and all guests should bring along an appropriate gift, in this case something for the kitchen or something blue.

They are usually held in the daytime, without elaborate food. In effect glorified girls'-talk sessions, brides' showers evolved from earlier days when a future bride might show her friends her trousseau and the things she had made and collected for her house.

If you are invited to a shower, you should take along a suitable gift, and write to thank the host afterwards.

Calamities

1 In case of a death, with indefinite postponement, an announcement and individual notices should be given:

   Because of the death of Mr William Shakespeare, Mr and Mrs John Jones regret they are cancelling/postponing the marriage of their daughter...

(If a new date is already arranged, put it in.)

2 Cancellation for other reasons:

   Mr and Mrs John Jones announce that the marriage of ... and ... will not now take place.

3 Any alteration should be imparted to guests at the earliest opportunity, since some may already have made long-distance travel plans. If the wedding is

cancelled completely then gifts should be returned to donors as quickly as possible.

4 Who ever breaks an engagement, nowadays the ring is generally considered to have been given unconditionally. You would perhaps return it only if it had been a family ring. Similarly, personal gifts (but not household articles) are deemed to have been given unconditionally.

5 Wedding or engagement presents are considered to have been made conditionally, and should be returned to the donors as soon as possible.

Chapter Two
THE DAY

Countdown to Start of Service

Plenty of Time Before
The bride makes sure she has her going-away clothes and all that she needs for her honeymoon suitably placed for changing at the reception. She may have her hair and make-up done. She gets dressed—she may arrange her veil over her face—and she should put her engagement ring on her right hand.

All members of the bridal party get dressed. The best man should check he has the ring (or rings, if bride and groom are to exchange them).

Minus 45 minutes
Ushers arrive at the church and give out service sheets. The bride's guests usually sit on the left of the church and the groom's guests on the right, with the families at the front in each case. If the division is unequal, however, suitably distribute guests other than family.

Minus 20 minutes
Groom and best man arrive and take their places at the front right-hand side. Guests should aim to arrive about this time. *(Note:* guests should avoid waving to Aunt Gladys across the aisle and talking in loud whispers. There will be plenty of time at the reception to catch up on news.)

Minus 10 minutes
Bride's mother arrives and is escorted to her place at the front left-hand side by one of the ushers. Bridesmaids arrive.

Minus 5 minutes

Bride and her father arrive, a few minutes early to allow for photographs and possible rearrangement of her veil and gown.

Service

The bride and her father* proceed up the aisle, the bride on her father's right arm. Attendants follow behind.

(front of procession)

(ring bearer and/or flower girl)

father & bride

attendants, singly or in pairs

(Note: the bride is traditionally given away by her father or another close relative, although sometimes her mother gives her away.)

As the bride and her father reach the groom, he and his best man step out so they form a quartet.

(altar)

father   bride   groom   best man

attendants

The bride turns and hands her bouquet to the chief bridesmaid.

The *exact service* will have been determined by the bride and groom in discussion with the minister beforehand. Each service is slightly different. What is common to all services is the question: 'Who giveth this woman to be married to this man?', at which point the father takes the bride's right hand and gives it to the minister, who passes it to the groom. Vows follow, with exchange of rings, and after this the bride's father takes his place next to the bride's mother at the front left-hand side of the church, and best man retreats to the front right-hand side.

The congregation may sing a hymn while the minister

communicates privately with the bride and groom. After a final blessing, the bridal party goes to the vestry for the *signing of the register*.

Two adult witnesses are required, so the minimum number going to the vestry consists of minister, bride and groom and two others. Often all members of the main bridal party are present. While the signing is taking place, music may be played.

Generally a fanfare of music heralds the emergence of the bride and groom. The exit procession follows this pattern:

(altar)

bride's father with groom's mother

groom's father with bride's mother

best man with chief bridesmaid

other attendants, singly or in pairs

groom & bride

(ring bearer and/or flower girl)

(front of procession)

After the bridal party has left the church, the guests can leave at leisure.

Do not have photographs taken directly outside the main church door, as it either prevents guests leaving or means Aunt Gladys will inadvertently appear in the pictures.

Everyone now goes on to the *reception* (see pages 17-31, 65).

Register Office

The ceremony will probably be slotted into a tight schedule, so it is important that everyone turns up in good time. (See page 15.)

The registrar will explain exactly what is going to happen. Bride, groom and witnesses simply have to follow instructions.

Afterwards, remember that there may be others waiting, so take yourselves off to the reception as soon as you can.

Reception

If there is a receiving line, this is the order:

(entry to reception)

bride's parents
groom's parents
bride
groom
attendants

Guests come in as couples—or families (it doesn't matter whether man or woman comes first). If there is a Master of Ceremonies, give your name clearly so that you can be 'announced' to the reception line.

If there is no Master of Ceremonies, it is a good idea to say your name clearly as you progress down the line. Everyone will then know who you are. You may want to kiss anyone you know well as you progress along the line. In other cases, give a quick firm handshake. Even if you have a lot to say, do not hold up progress, as there will be others behind you waiting to be received. Keep any long conversations for a later occasion.

At the end of the reception line there may be a waiter holding a tray of drinks. If not, look around to find out where the bar is—but do not rush towards it with Olympic haste.

You will probably have lots of drinking time now before any food is served. *Go slow!*

If you do not have anyone to talk to, go up and introduce yourself to other people. Everyone is there for the same reason, so find out how other guests know the bride and/or groom. No-one will introduce you: it is up to you and there may be many others in the same boat, not knowing anyone else there.

Food
This may be a large sit-down meal or a buffet—or just light snacks. You will soon discover what the form is (see pages 19-22).

Cutting the Cake
This is the traditional part of all receptions. The bride and groom together ceremonially make the first cut, with the groom's hand over that of his bride.

The cake-cutting is usually heralded by a summons from the Master of Ceremonies, or else someone with a bell or a loud voice will call for everyone's attention.

The cake-cutting ceremony precedes the speeches.

Speeches
(See suggestions for speeches on pages 30-31).

You may be asked to speak if you are:

1 An old friend (or the father) of the bride, proposing the health of the bride and groom.
2 The groom, responding and thanking the bride's parents, his parents and anyone else relevant, and proposing a toast to the bridesmaids.
3 The best man, replying on the bridesmaids' behalf and perhaps at this point reading out any messages sent in.

Person by Person
(alphabetically)

Attendants
There is often a chief bridesmaid, whose particular role on the day is to:

1 Help the bride to dress.
2 Supervise any smaller attendants during the ceremony (and later at the reception).
3 Give last-minute touches to the bride as she arrives at the church.

4 Take the bride's bouquet as she arrives at the altar—and hold it until after the signing of the register, when it is given back to the bride for the final exit procession.

5 Help the bride to change into her going-away outfit.

6 After she has gone, look after the wedding clothes.

Other attendants generally look pretty, act nicely and help in any way they can. A ring bearer and/or flower girl (if appropriate) precedes the bride and her father up the aisle, and bride and groom down the aisle. The American custom is for the ring bearer to hand the ring to the best man, who will, in turn, give it to the minister at the appropriate moment.

Best man
Beforehand, the best man traditionally:

1 Makes sure that the groom will get to the church on time (in other words, he prevents the organization of an enormous stag party the previous night).

2 Checks that all arrangements are under way, and that ushers have the right clothes, buttonholes will turn up, and printed service sheets are delivered.

3 Considers—in discussion with the ushers—car-parking arrangements and transport between service and reception.

On the day, he:

1 Makes sure that he has the ring(s).

2 Makes sure the groom's going-away clothes are ready at reception venue.

3 Makes sure that the groom is correctly dressed.

4 Accompanies the groom to the church, to arrive 20 minutes before the service begins.

5 At the appropriate part of the ceremony, hands the rings to the minister.

6 Pays the minister and any musician/choir fees.

7 Supervises the reception, liaising with the toast-master and, possibly, reading out telegrams. It is the best man who actually times the reception and decides when the cake should be cut, and when the bride and groom should go and change.

8 Makes a speech, responding to the toast of the bridesmaids.

Afterwards, the best man is responsible for returning the groom's wedding clothes, and for making sure nothing is left behind at the reception.

Bride's father

Although he may not have been involved to a great extent with prior arrangements for the wedding, on the day itself the bride's father comes into his own.

It is normally he who gives his daughter away, and if she must radiate happiness, he must look his best, too. Many fathers of brides bitterly resent the prospect of giving up their weekly golf but, when the day arrives, they thoroughly enjoy it and realize that instead of losing a daughter they are gaining a son.

This is also the day when the bride's father sees many old friends.

Note: to help ease her parents' post-wedding blues, a bride might arrange for them to go out to a surprise dinner for two. Or, alternatively, why not arrange for someone to come into the house during their absence at the reception and leave a bottle of their favourite champagne in an ice bucket, with two glasses and a little personal note?

Bride's mother

This should be her day off, but, in practice, it generally turns out to be an extremely tiring day. Last-minute telephones calls, houseguests, perhaps an emotional daughter, and a myriad of other problems, can make the wedding a demanding experience.

Once the bride's mother gets to the church (ten minutes before the service), she can certainly relax. She has no legal part to play in the ceremony, though she may well accompany the party to the signing of the register. At the reception, she normally stands in the receiving line.

Note: the bride's mother should avoid wearing any large rings. Shaking hands with masses of well-wishers in the reception line can be quite painful!

Friend of the bride
Usually an older friend who has known the bride for many years, he is chosen because of his ability to make a suitable speech. He, in particular, should avoid embarrassing anecdotes.

Groom's parents
They are spared any responsibility today. They should, however, consider themselves very special people, as without them, the groom would not be there!

They can also be tremendously helpful at the reception, looking after their guests, not hitherto known to the bride's family. Regardless of whether or not they have helped pay for the reception, to all intents they have no traditional function today, other than possibly stand in the receiving line at the reception (see page 65). They should do what they can to help, discreetly and without fuss.

Guests
Guests should aim to turn up about 20 minutes before the service is due to start.

In some countries (such as the United States) it is customary to bring gifts with you. Leave them in the car during the service. When you go to the reception, there will be a table to put your gift on, or someone will take it from you. Make sure it is well labelled. The bride may well not open it until her return from honeymoon, and she will want to know who it is from!

Guests should dress suitably. If you are unsure, ask the bride's mother, when replying to the invitation, what the dress will be. Guests can wear clothes similar to peripheral members of the bridal party, and all the same points apply (see page 43).

It is generally considered in poor taste to take

photographs or make recordings during the service, unless prior permission has been obtained. It is quite all right to take equipment with you so that you can record after the service.

Avoid making a show of yourself during the service. It is not *your* day. Join in the singing—but not out of tune, and try not to fall asleep.

At the reception, watch your alcohol intake. If you do not want to eat, don't. If you do not want a piece of wedding cake, however, it would be courteous to ask if you can have your piece wrapped in a napkin so that you can 'eat it later'.

Ushers

Several ushers should be delegated beforehand, and it is a good idea for the best man to organize a meeting, so that everyone knows what is going to happen.

Ushers are responsible on the day for greeting people at the church, giving out order sheets and showing guests to appropriate places. After the service, they see that everyone has transport to the reception.

They then make sure the church is left tidy. They should take away all service sheets and, if necessary, help clean up confetti.

Chapter Three
AFTERWARDS

Immediately after the wedding it is necessary for someone—best man and chief bridesmaid, perhaps—to check that all gifts have been carefully stored and that all clothes and other personal items belonging to the bride and groom have been taken away.

The reception host—probably the bride's father—will want to check catering accounts and, to hold his name in good stead, he should settle the bill as soon as possible.

The bride's mother may want to write thank-you notes to all who helped. A sample letter (handwritten, please) could be as follows:

Seven Oaks
14 February 19—

Dear Miss Tibbs,

I do want to thank you so much for working specially on Saturday morning so that Eloise's bouquet—and those of her little attendants—could be absolutely fresh. I know you do not normally work over weekends and we all appreciated what you did.

Everyone commented on the flowers. They were lovely. Thank you for helping to make Eloise's day so special.
With all good wishes

Sincerely,
Mary Smith

Wills

A will automatically becomes invalid on marriage (or remarriage). You should make a new one as soon as possible to avoid intestacy, in which case the law would decide how your estate should be distributed.

Passports

The groom will not need to have his passport altered—but the bride should, if she is travelling abroad on her honeymoon or in the immediate future. If you ask for a passport in your married name before the wedding, it can be sent to the minister to give to you on the day.

Guests

It is a nice custom for guests to write personal thank-yous to the bride's parents (or whoever gave the wedding). A short note making some nice comment about the occasion will suffice, and will make the hosts feel that all their expense and trouble was appreciated.

Chapter Four
SPECIAL WEDDINGS

Note: every wedding is unique, and the recipes below can be combined. Perhaps you live in Banff and your partner-to-be in Bude. Perhaps he has been married before. You will therefore find the information on far-apart weddings and second weddings of particular help to you.

Executive Weddings

One feature of the current emergence of equality is that professional women often marry later. In 1982, for instance, 12% of American women in the 30-34 age group had not married (double the number in a 1970 census).

Achieving, professional women are transforming the tradition of marriage. As Dr Ruth Neubauer, former president of the New York State Association of Marriage and Family Therapy, says, 'Increasingly they wait longer to get married and are getting their curiosity out of their systems first. Once people have done this, they settle down to one person. People are living together first and then they either break up or make it permanent.'

Beverly Stephen, writing in the June 1984 issue of *American Working Woman,* said that she feels there is surprisingly little difference between the planning of an advertising campaign and a wedding. You set it all up logically and without fuss. 'The wedding should not be planned on company time,' she says. 'Do not expect your professional staff to assist: your secretary should not be asked to address the invitations.'

Keeping wedding plans away from the office saves having to invite 'the office gang'. Obviously, your 'boss' and relevant superiors should be told, but as far as everyone else is concerned the bride-to-be may simply be going on her usual holiday, from which she returns wearing a wedding ring.

Lack of time means that many executive brides hand over all the planning to someone else. If this is your mother, make sure she accepts the fact that it is your wedding and not hers. You do not want to end up wearing the dress of *her* dreams, with a guest list consisting solely of her bridge buddies.

An executive bride may well feel happiest in a simple dress that can be worn afterwards (see some of the ideas in the section on second marriages). On the other hand, she may, for once in her life, prefer a traditional gown (see pages 37-41).

Does the bride change her name professionally on marriage? This is a personal choice and depends on such features as:

1 Her name beforehand.
2 Her husband's name.
3 Whether or not she was well known professionally before marriage.
4 How seriously she wants to bring her marriage into her professional life.

Gifts

What should you give the executive bride, who probably already has everything and is short of time, so that elaborate pasta-makers do not fit the bill? How about a case of wine, a telephone answering machine or a mini-television?

Famous Weddings

Someone in the public eye must choose whether to be married in private or in public.

If a private wedding is chosen, make sure it *is* private. I remember having lunch at Eaton's, in Belgravia, at the next table to the party following the marriage of two television stars. They did not seem to have announced the event to the press, and they were able to have a really quiet and enjoyable party.

By comparison, those who do choose a 'public wedding' must be prepared for the public to take an interest. This means, today, television cameras, videos and the whole razzmatazz of modern technology. Mick Jagger (sneakers and all) and Bianca Jagger knew that their wedding would be in all the next day's papers around the world, as did Bjorn Borg and his Romanian bride Marianna.

If you are invited to a 'famous wedding' and you know it is a private event, do *not* contact the press. If, on the other hand, you know it will be a public beano, be prepared for the crowds. Make sure you take your invitation along, to avoid being turned away as a gatecrasher.

Far-Apart Weddings

If future bride and groom live a long distance apart, it may be easier for one to do all the wedding planning. During my own year-long engagement, my fiancé was in Beirut. I was in Wiltshire. We did meet at Christmas (in England) and Easter (Lebanon) but in between I did all the planning. In fact, it helped me pass the time!

If you have to plan a wedding all on your own, it is a tremendous help to have someone, a mother or older sister or good friend, on whose advice you can rely.

Handicapped Weddings

Before contemplating marriage, a handicapped person will want to discuss in detail with the future spouse, and with doctors and specialists, the feasibility of marriage.

From a sexual point of view, there are marvellously helpful organizations to contact (National Association for Mental Health, and Sexual and Personal Relationships of the Disabled, for instance).

Talk to your local minister and to good friends. Try and spend plenty of time together before you finally make up your mind. Can you — both — cope?

(Incidentally, there is no reason why a handicapped person cannot be a bridesmaid. It may be easier for her to use a wheelchair rather than struggle to make her own way, in which case the wheelchair can be attractively decorated. The bride could consider having an extra adult attendant to help with the bridesmaid — and also give extra attention to the bride.)

Mixed-Religion Weddings

If a Church of England believer marries a Roman Catholic the marriage can be held in a Catholic church, but the couple should establish beforehand in what religion any children will be brought up. It may be possible to marry in the Church of England, perhaps with a Roman Catholic priest contributing to an ecumenical 'mixed marriage'. You should talk to your local priest.

If a Christian marries a Jew, a synagogue blessing following the civil ceremony is not possible. Converts recognized by a Jewish court may be able to marry in a synagogue.

Anyone who plans to marry someone from a different religion and culture should consider very carefully the problems that may arise. I remember a woman friend of mine, many years ago, all set to marry a foreign doctor. She flew out to meet the family before the wedding, came back to London and promptly called the wedding off. She had seen (as I had so many times) the difficulties brides could later encounter in a mixed-religion, mixed-race marriage.

No-Family Weddings

No family around? You must have friends. Ask someone close to you to 'give you away'. If there is no-one to host the reception for you, host it yourselves.

No friends? Well, at the worst you only need two

witnesses, and there will probably be a couple nearby whom you can ask.

No-Money Weddings

Never mind. Have a simple wedding. Admit that you are doing it 'on the cheap', and ask the guests to bring along their own food and drink for a marvellous picnic. Make it simple and do not try to be pretentious. No-one will appreciate engraved invitations and champagne throughout the reception if you have had to mortgage everything to do it.

No-Time Weddings

Here there are various alternatives:

1 Ask someone to do all the arrangements for you (see executive weddings).
2 Make the wedding as simple as possible.
3 If you have no time and no money, make it *very* simple.

Overseas Weddings

If you are getting married overseas, find out about local customs beforehand—and do as they do. In America, for instance, the main speeches may be at a family dinner the night before the wedding. In New Zealand, a wedding may well be performed by a Justice of the Peace in your own garden, say around 4 p.m., with a dance afterwards.

If you are in doubt about local customs of another country, approach the embassy or consulate of that country.

Pregnant Weddings

Be honest! Everyone can count to nine. Nowadays it makes much more sense to say 'Yes, we *are* having a baby, and we are getting married on...'. Emphasize the positive. The baby will be born legitimate.

If the bride is heavily pregnant, thank goodness for the custom of carrying a floral bouquet. Have a larger spray than you would otherwise choose!

Register Office Weddings
See page 64.

Second Weddings
The question of whether or not you can be married in church may depend on your local vicar. The Bishop of London, for example, regulates that 'An incumbent may...offer prayers in church with those who have contracted civil marriage'. If you want to have a Service of Blessing you should first talk to your local vicar. If he is unable to help you, go to the next stage (in the Church of England, the Rural Dean).

A certain amount of tact is necessary when organizing a second (or third) wedding. A bride who has been married before should not wear full flowing white, and guest lists should be carefully selected in order not to embarrass anyone. A general rule is that as soon as a wedding is planned and a church service is wanted, the bride and groom should immediately go in person to talk to the minister.

At the service or ceremony itself, the groom should dress up or down suitably to complement the bride.

Unusual Weddings
Quite honestly, it is not usual for a man of 70 to marry a woman of 22, nor indeed for a woman of 70 to marry a man of 22... Neither is it acceptable (except perhaps in San Francisco) for a man to 'marry' a man or a woman 'marry' a woman.

If you want an unusual relationship to be blessed and recognized, go and talk to your minister to see what he or she advises.

If you are invited to an 'unusual' wedding, remember that you have been asked to help celebrate the joining of those two persons' lives. Whatever your private opinion may be, try to think of *their* feelings.

MY WEDDING NOTES

Date...

Place..

Time of service...

Place of reception...

Bridal Party

Bride
Name, address and telephone numbers (day,
evening)...
....
....

Groom
Name, address and telephone numbers (day,
evening)...
....
....

Best Man
Name, address and telephone numbers (day,
evening)...
....
....

Attendants
Name, address and telephone numbers (day,
evening)...
....
....

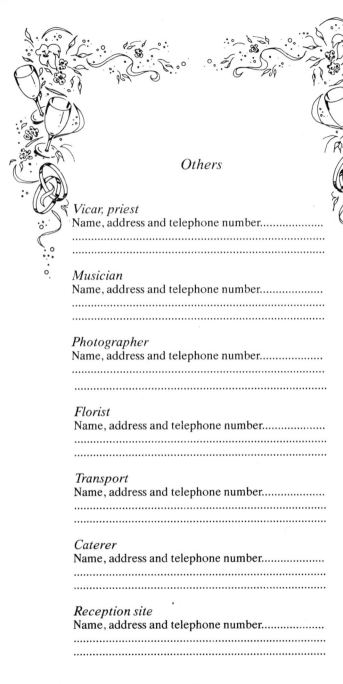

Others

Vicar, priest
Name, address and telephone number....................
....
....

Musician
Name, address and telephone number....................
....
....

Photographer
Name, address and telephone number....................
....
....

Florist
Name, address and telephone number....................
....
....

Transport
Name, address and telephone number....................
....
....

Caterer
Name, address and telephone number....................
....
....

Reception site
Name, address and telephone number....................
....
....

Honeymoon site
Name, address and telephone number...................
....
....

Bride's Outfit

Sizes: dress...

bra..

shoes...

(contact, name/phone)

Dress..

Veil..

Shoes...

Bra...

Tights/stockings...

Hair details..

Make-up details...

Flowers...

Going-away outfit...

Groom's Outfit

Sizes: jacket...

trousers: waist...

outer leg..

inner leg...

shoes..

hat..

Jacket...

Trousers..

Tie..

Shirt..

Shoes..

Buttonhole...

Hat..

Attendants' Outfits

(make separate list for each)

Sizes: dress..

      bra...

      shoes..

(contact, name/phone)

Dress...

Shoes..

Bra..

Tights/stockings...

Hair details..

Make-up details..

Flowers..

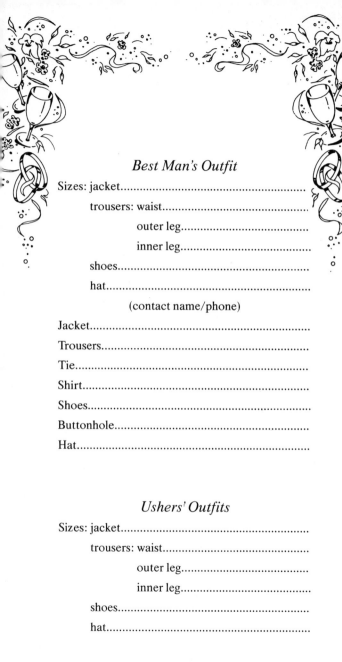

Best Man's Outfit

Sizes: jacket...

       trousers: waist...

               outer leg...

               inner leg...

       shoes...

       hat...

(contact name/phone)

Jacket..

Trousers...

Tie...

Shirt..

Shoes...

Buttonhole...

Hat..

Ushers' Outfits

Sizes: jacket...

       trousers: waist...

               outer leg...

               inner leg...

       shoes...

       hat...

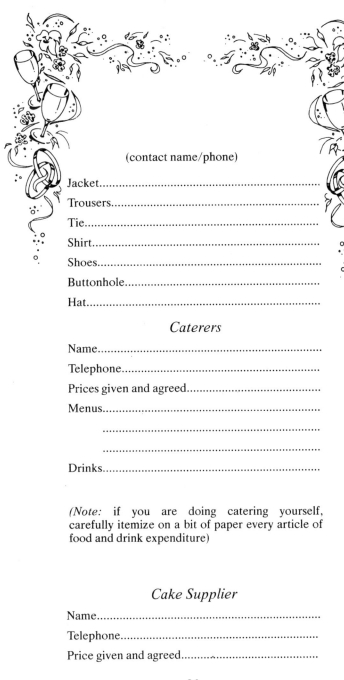

(contact name/phone)

Jacket..

Trousers..

Tie..

Shirt...

Shoes..

Buttonhole..

Hat...

Caterers

Name...

Telephone..

Prices given and agreed...

Menus...

....

....

Drinks...

(Note: if you are doing catering yourself, carefully itemize on a bit of paper every article of food and drink expenditure)

Cake Supplier

Name...

Telephone..

Price given and agreed...

86

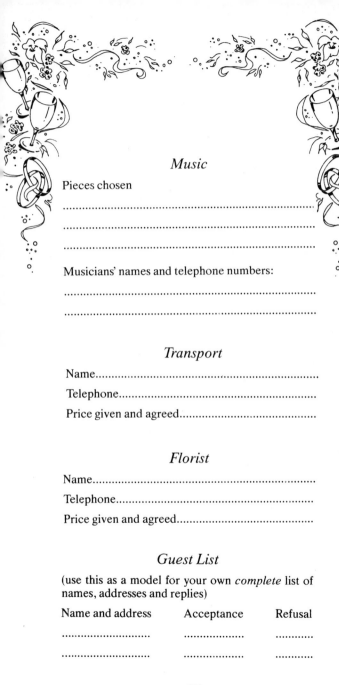

Music

Pieces chosen

....

....

....

Musicians' names and telephone numbers:

....

....

Transport

Name..

Telephone...

Price given and agreed.......................................

Florist

Name..

Telephone...

Price given and agreed.......................................

Guest List

(use this as a model for your own *complete* list of
names, addresses and replies)

Name and address	Acceptance	Refusal
....	....	....
....	....	....

Present List

(use this as a model for a complete list)

From	Item	Thank-you written
....	....	....
....	....	....
....	....	....
....	....	....
....	....	....
....	....	....
....	....	....
....	....	....
....	....	....
....	....	....
....	....	....
....	....	....
....	....	....
....	....	....

USEFUL READING

Magazines

Brides

Modern Brides

Books

'Best Man', *Marriage Etiquette*, Foulsham 1974

Dobson, Sue, *The Wedding Day Book*, Arrow 1981

Nissen, Richard (ed.), *The Romantic Weekend Book: Perfect Places for that Special Weekend*, Futura 1984

Spencer, Ivor, *Speeches and Toasts*, Ward Lock 1980

Wade, John, *It's Your Turn to Speak*, Batsford 1985

USEFUL ADDRESSES

Britain

Champagne Bureau, 14 Pall Mall, London SW1Y 5LU.
Tel. *(01) 839 1461*

Debenham's, Princes Street, Edinburgh EH1.
Tel. *(031) 225 1320*

Embassy Hotels, 34 Queen's Gate, London SW7 5JA.
Tel. *(01) 581 3466*

Harrods, Knightsbridge, London SW1X 7XL.
Tel. *(01) 730 1234*

Ivor Spencer School for British Butlers and
Administrators, 12 Little Bournes, Alleyn Park,
London SE21 8SE. Tel. *(01) 670 5585*

Moët & Chandon (London) Ltd, 13 Grosvenor
Crescent, London SW1X 7EE. Tel. *(01) 235 9411*

National Association for Mental Health (MIND),
22 Harley Street, London W1N 1AP. Tel. *(01) 637 0741*

The Passport Office, Clive House, Petty France,
London SW1H 9E. Tel. (surnames A-D) *(01) 213 3344;*
(surnames E-K) *(01) 213 7272;* (surnames L-Q)
(01) 213 6161; (surnames R-Z) *(01) 213 3434*

United States

Champagne News & Information Bureau, 220 E42 St, NYC, NY 10017. Tel. *212 907 9382*

Moët & Chandon in US:
Schieffelin & Co., 30 Cooper Square, NYC, NY 10003. Tel. *212 477 7025*

The Passport Office
(1) 270 Rockefeller Center, 630 Fifth Avenue, NYC, NY 10020. Tel. *212 541 7710*
(2) 1425 K St NW, Washington DC 20524.
Tel. *202 783 8170*
and:
Boston *617 223 3831*
Chicago *312 353 7155*
Los Angeles *213 536 6503*
San Francisco *415 556 2630*

Neiman-Marcus, PO 2968, Dallas Tx75221.
Tel. *214 823 7939*

For further information on many things mentioned in this book, and for details of Mary Gostelow Enterprises and The Complete Woman, please send two first class stamps to:

Mary Gostelow (GM), PO Box 135, Ringwood, Hants BH24 1JB

INDEX